AF316799

THE RELATIONSHIP OF THE MOON AND THE TIDES

ENVIRONMENT BOOKS FOR KIDS

Children's Environment Books

In this book, we're going to talk about the relationship between the Moon and the tides. So, let's get right to it!

WHAT ARE TIDES?

If you've spent any length of time by the water, you've noticed that the level of the water in relationship to the shore varies throughout the day. This pattern of water rising and then falling and rising again is called the tides.

Winter storm over ocean with rough seas.

WHAT CAUSES THE TIDES?

The forces of gravity of the Sun and the Moon cause the levels of water on the Earth to change. As the Earth rotates, its gravity pulls the water inward but, at the same time, centrifugal force pushes it outward. This inward and outward pull of forces keeps the water at about equal levels around the planet.

However, the pull of the Moon on the Earth is strong enough to change the levels of the water on Earth and this is what creates the ebb and flow of the tides.

Approaching storm over the ocean.

Full moon over the ocean

THE MOON'S GRAVITATIONAL PULL

The Moon is close enough to the Earth that its gravitational pull affects us. Water is fluid and not attached to the Earth like mountains are. The gravitational pull of the Moon makes the water on the side of the Earth facing the Moon to bulge off the face of the planet. As the Moon travels around the Earth and as the Earth spins on its axis, the bulge moves to wherever the Moon and the Earth face each other.

To see this, draw a picture of a circle to represent the Earth. Then, draw the Moon directly above it on your sheet of paper. Where the Earth faces the Moon it will be high tide. Let's label that direction north. Then, the areas of the Earth that will be experiencing low tide will be the east and west. What about the side of the Earth farthest away from the Moon? Surprisingly, this side is at high tide as well. In our drawing, this would be the south direction.

CENTRIFUGAL FORCE

The water on the side of Earth farthest from the Moon also bulges out creating high tide, but this time it's for a totally different reason. It's due to centrifugal force.

Imagine that you have a very heavy object that's tied to a rope. You swing it around your body while you're rotating. As you swing the rope, you find yourself leaning back to balance.

Big stormy wave at night

The center of mass lies between your body and the object you're swinging. It feels like the heavy object wants to fly off, but it can't because it's attached to the rope.

In the gravitational system of the Earth and Moon, gravity is similar to the rope. It pulls to keep the two bodies together, while centrifugal force works to keep them apart. On the Earth's opposite side, the centrifugal force is greater than the Moon's forceful pull so that ocean water bulges out as if it could escape Earth's gravity.

Ocean Tides.

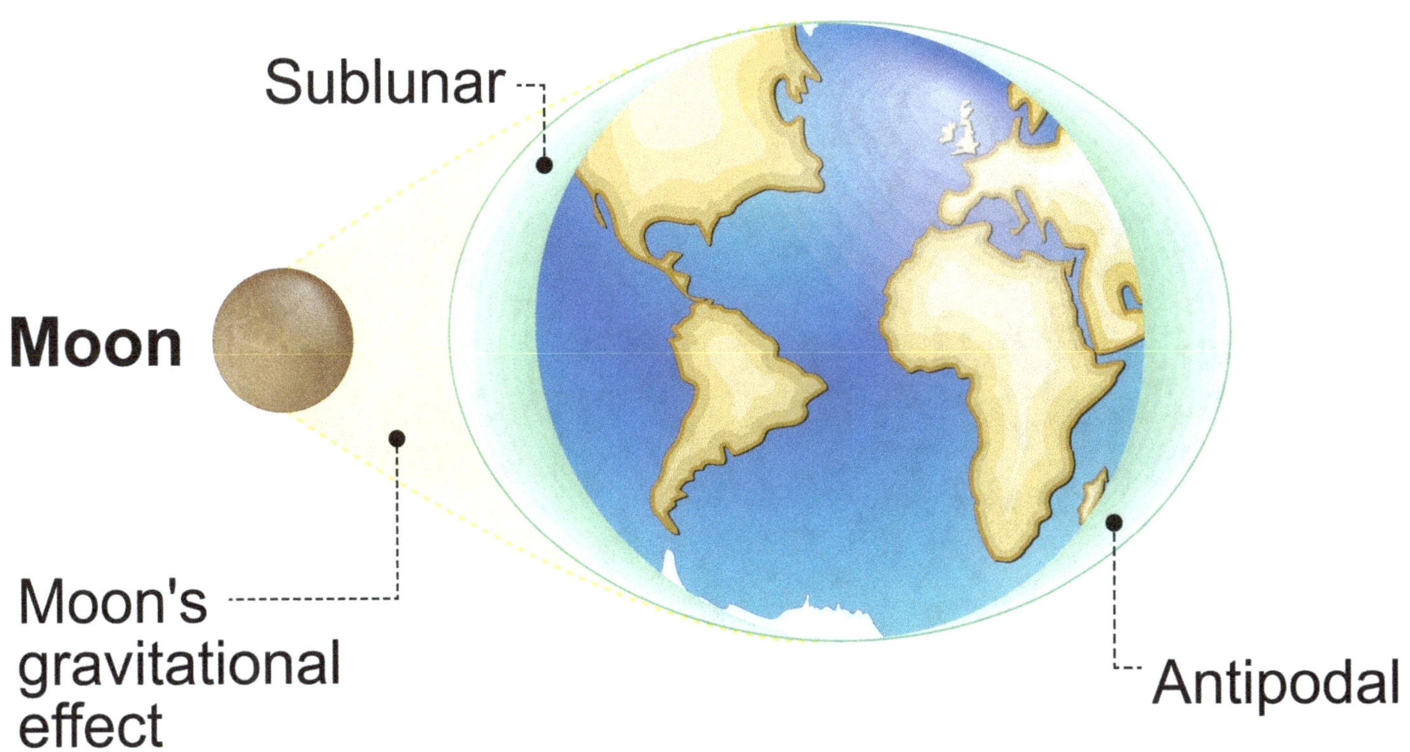

Sublunar
Moon
Moon's
gravitational
effect
Antipodal

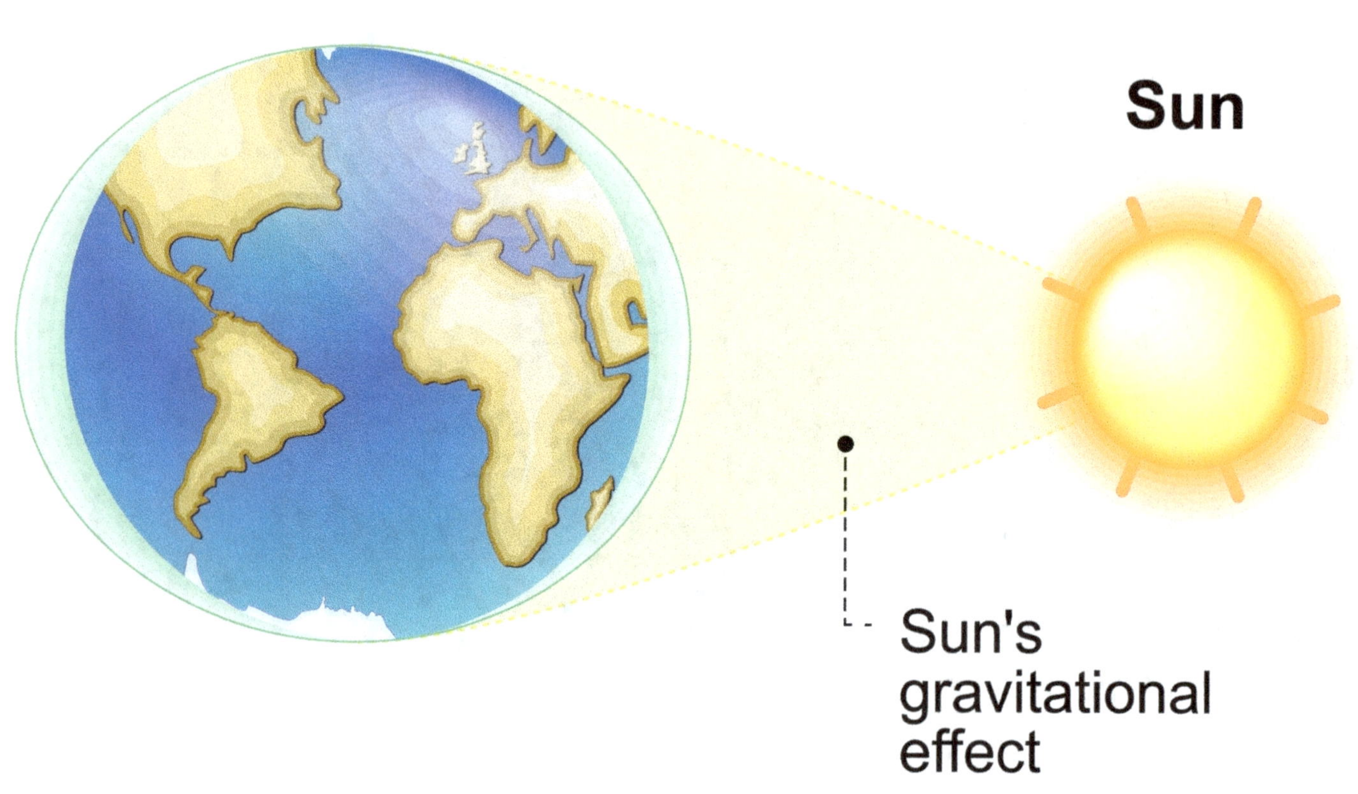
Sun
Sun's
gravitational
effect

THE SUN'S GRAVITATIONAL PULL

The same forces are at work with the gravitational pull of the Sun. The Sun's pull causes water to go in its direction. Likewise, as before, the centrifugal force caused by the revolution of the Earth and the Sun causes the water on Earth's opposite side to bulge. High tide happens there as well.

Ocean Tides.

Even though the gravitational pull of the Sun is much greater than that of the Moon, the Moon is much closer to Earth, so the Sun doesn't have as much impact as the force of the Moon on Earth's tides. If you take the distance from the Earth to the Moon and multiply it by 380 times, this result would be the distance the Earth is from the Sun, so that's why the Sun doesn't have as much pull in this situation.

Oceans Tides.

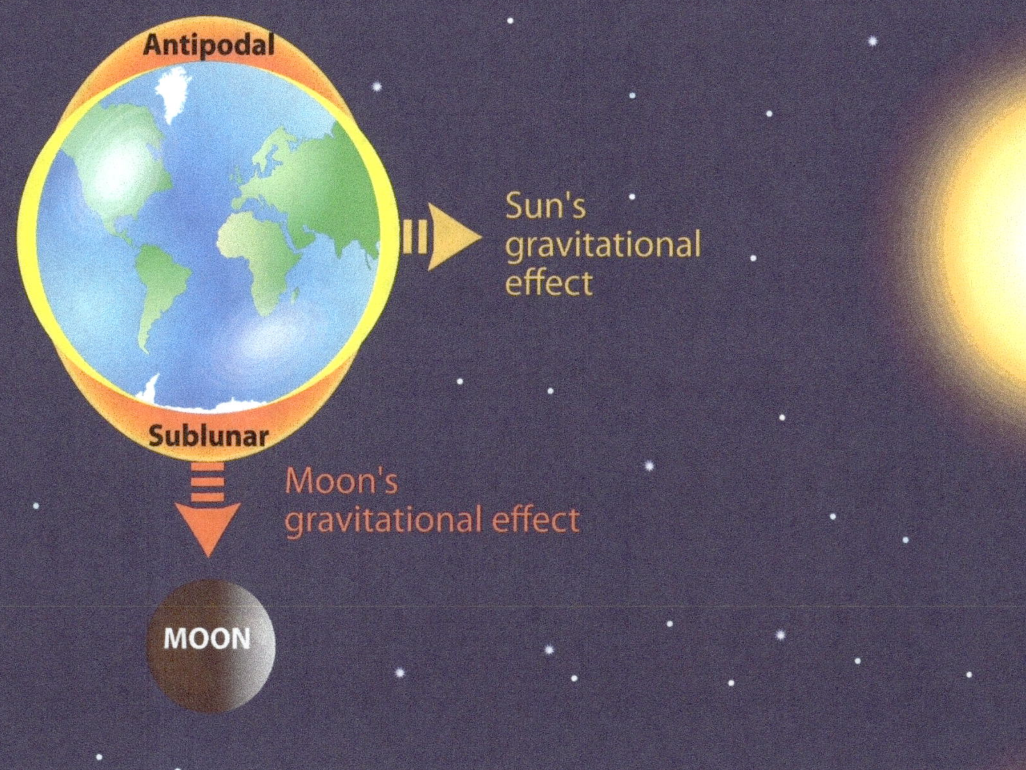

Antipodal
Sun's gravitational effect
Sublunar
Moon's gravitational effect
MOON
SUN

High tide
MOON
Low tide
SUN

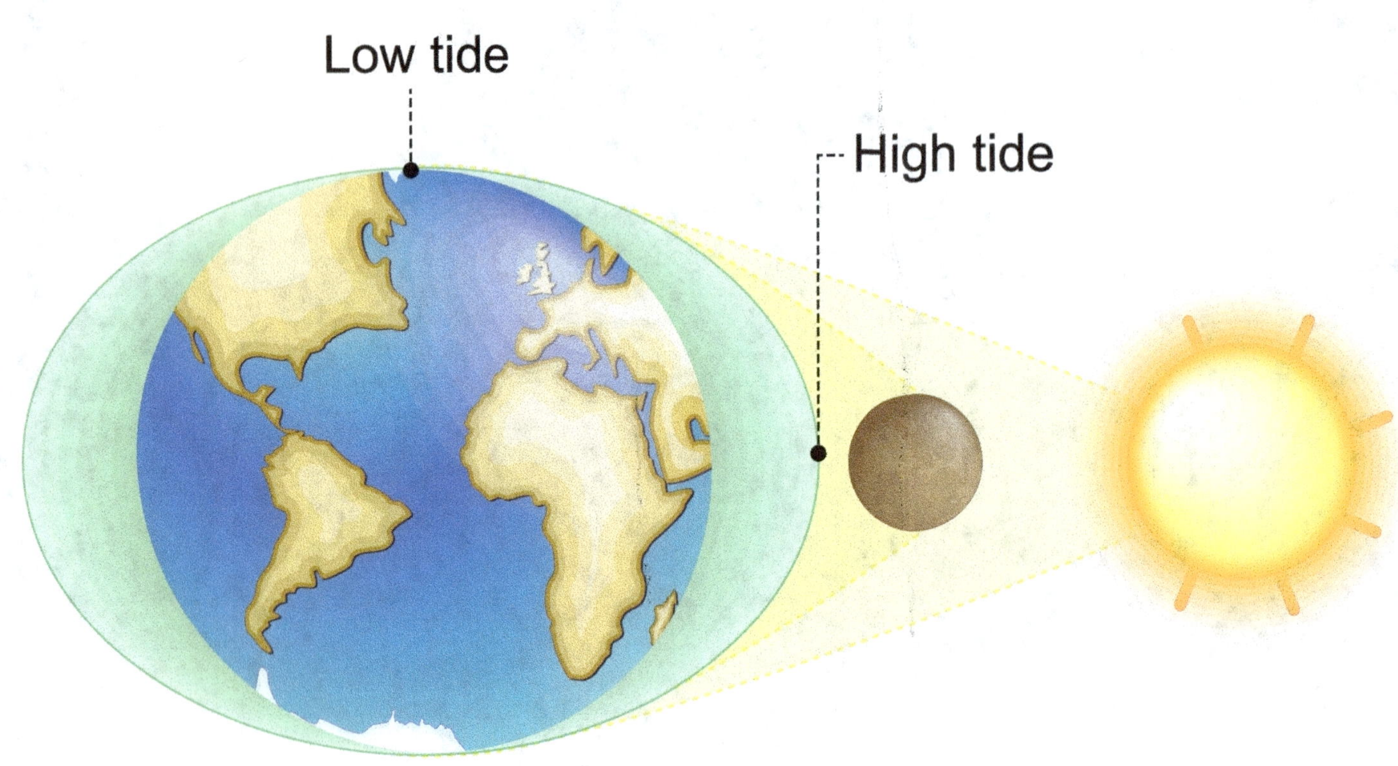

Low tide
High tide

WHEN THE SUN AND THE MOON LINE UP

When the Sun and Moon line up, it enhances the gravitational pull of the Moon. The Sun is giving Moon's pull a little boost, so the tides increase. This alignment happens during the phases of the New Moon and also the Full Moon. There's a name for this alignment. It's called syzygy. These types of tides are called spring tides, not because they happen in the spring, but because they make the tides spring up a little higher than normal.

Ocean Tides.

WHEN THE SUN AND THE MOON ARE AT 90-DEGREE ANGLES

During the phases of the First or Third Quarter Moon, from a location on Earth, the Sun and Moon are at 90-degree angles to each other. During this half-moon phase, the high tides don't measure as high as they would under normal circumstances.

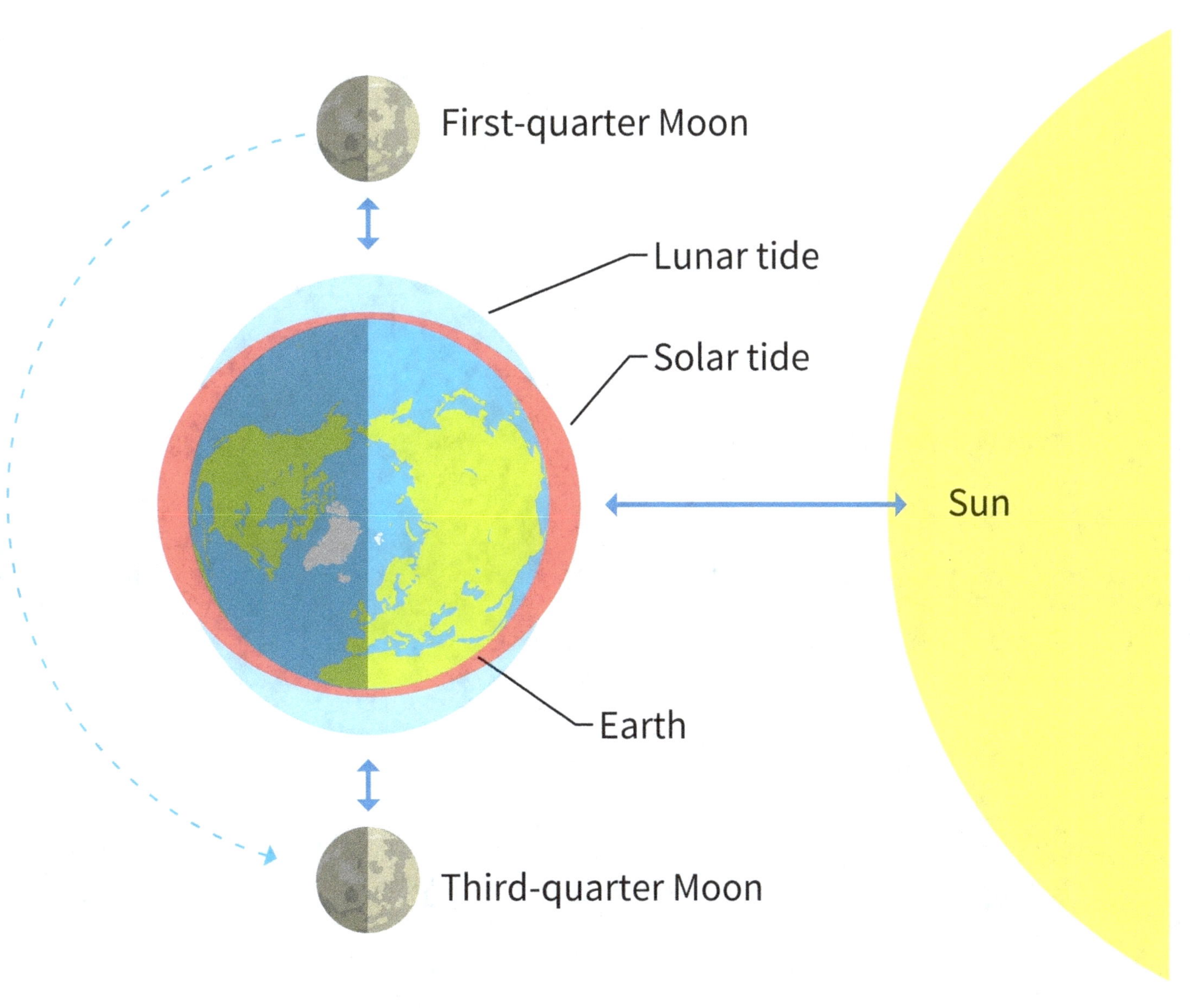

First-quarter Moon
Lunar tide
Solar tide
Sun
Earth
Third-quarter Moon

This is because the Sun still exerts some force, even though it's so far away. It decreases the influence of the Moon's gravitational pull. The lower resulting tides are named neap tides.

DISTANCE OF THE MOON TO THE EARTH

The Moon isn't always the same exact distance from the Earth. When the orbit of the Moon brings it closer to Earth, that cycle is perigee, and when it's further away, that cycle is apogee. When it's closest, its force is sometimes 50% greater so the height of the tides reflects that. When it's farthest away, the tides still occur, but their height is less tall than usual.

Moonrise over the Pacific Ocean at night.

HOW OFTEN DOES THE CYCLE OF TIDES OCCUR?

Tides occur in either a diurnal or semi-diurnal pattern. In a diurnal pattern, they happen twice a day. In a semi-diurnal pattern they happen as two high tides and two low tides per day. It seems like these should happen like clockwork, every 24 hours, but that isn't the case.

Sky, waterline and underwater

The reason is that the Moon takes longer than 24 hours to line up with the same point on Earth. It takes about 24 hours plus 50 more minutes each time, so the tides are staggered throughout the month.

OTHER FACTORS THAT INFLUENCE THE TIDES

Scientists can't calculate the tides simply by astronomy. That's because, in addition to these forces, the physical composition of the Earth and oceans impacts the tides as well. The angular height of the Moon above the Earth's equator makes a difference in its gravitational pull. Also the specific coastline's geography and the water's depth make a difference as well. The physical features or topography of the ocean floor also impact tides.

Current Tide at Saltstraumen in Norway.

Crisscross Waves.

THE CYCLES OF A TIDE

The tide ebbs and then flows throughout the day and night. The cycle goes like this:

- The level of the water rises.

- High tide occurs when the maximum height of the water has been reached.

- The level of the water dissipates.

- Low tide occurs when the height of the water is at its lowest.

- The cycle begins again.

TIDAL CURRENTS

The movement of the water can be described as flows of different types of currents.

FLOOD CURRENTS

When the water is rushing toward the shore, the currents can be described as flood currents.

Storm flood.

EBB CURRENTS

When the water is rushing away from the shore, the currents can be described as ebb currents.

SLACK WATER

At the precise time of either type of tides, high or low, there isn't a current. The water can be described as slack water.

Ebb Tide.

TIDAL RANGE

The tidal range is different in different areas. The tidal range is the difference in measurement when you compare high tide and low tide. The Sun's and Moon's forces as well as all the physical features of the location will have an impact on the tidal range.

Ocean tides.

Tidal range
High tide
Low tide

If you measure the tidal range in the open ocean, it's generally about 2 feet. However, along some coastlines the range is much greater. The greatest tidal range occurs off the coast of Canada at the Bay of Fundy. Tidal ranges there vary by 40 feet from low tide to high tide!

Low tide on the beach.

Tidal pool in the Wadden Sea at sunrise.

FASCINATING FACTS ABOUT TIDES

- The forces that impact tides also impact the shape of the Earth as well. They cause it to transform its shape by a few inches when the gravitational pull is strong.

- There are usually two spring and two neap tides every month.

- During a semidiurnal cycle, the low and high tide occur about 6 hours and 13 minutes from each other.

- Local weather can have an impact on tides as well as the larger astronomical forces.

- Green energy can be harnessed from the tides to create electricity. Tidal turbines or fences are used to generate the power.

- The locks of the Panama Canal help to raise or lower traveling ships from the two oceans. The tidal range in the Atlantic and Pacific Oceans is different.

Sandy beach in Thailand.

- The first scientist to figure out the connection between the Moon and tides was the astronomer Seleucus in 150 BC.

- Boats and ships can be damaged if they get stranded somewhere during low tide.

Awesome! Now you know more about the way the Moon affects the tides. You can find more Environment books from Baby Professor by searching the website of your favorite book retailer.

Visit

BABY PROFESSOR
EDUCATION KIDS

www.BabyProfessorBooks.com

to download Free Baby Professor eBooks
and view our catalog of new and exciting
Children's Books